MARBLE
PAINTING

Project Book

Learn how to create marble
decor for your home

10 projects inside

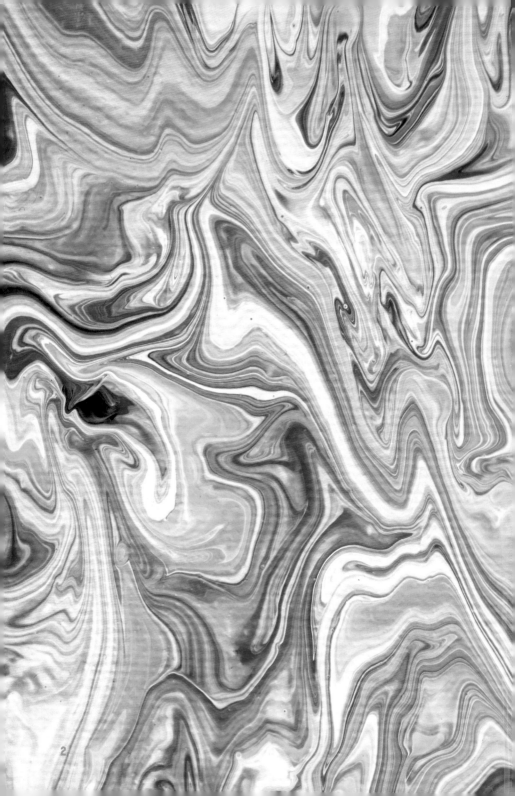

The joy of marbling lies in the excitement and unpredictability of the end result. No matter how many times you try, marbling will never be the same twice.

Be warned, with thousands of vibrant colour combinations to use and multiple items you can marble onto, it can become highly addictive!

In this book, we will teach you the process of marbling and give you all of the tips and tricks to marble like an expert.

KIT CONTENTS

WHAT'S INCLUDED:

6 x smooth pebbles
Wooden stirring stick
3 x acrylic paints

BASIC EQUIPMENT:

Marbling is relatively easy to do and,
if using the techniques in this book,
you will not need much additional
equipment.

We have provided all of the basic
items. All you will need is something to
put your water and acrylic paints into.
This can be anything that is waterproof
- you just need to make sure it's big
enough for your marbled items to fit
into, like a waterproof tray or bowl.

MARBLE PAINTING BASICS

MARBLING - THE BASICS

There are many different marbling techniques to choose from, such as alcohol inks and nail polish. In this set, we will be marbling pebbles using acrylic paints, this is super easy to do.

But don't worry, we have many more projects included, so you can learn the different types of marbling techniques.

TOP TIPS:

Sinking Paint

While there are a number of marbling techniques, some use water. This method requires the paint to float on the top. Occasionally, the paint can sink to the bottom, which prevents the marbling from working.

If you find this happening you have a few options;

1. When you drop your paint into the water, try not to use big drops. You want the paint to be as thin as possible so give the paint a good stir and pour really slowly.

2. If it still isn't working, you may need to add water to your paint. You can try different ratios but we suggest 1:1 water and paint. Give it a really good stir before trying to pour into your bowl or water again.

3. Mix your water with corn starch. We explain how to do this later.

4. Corn starch

Corn starch is a good way of ensuring the acrylic paint stays on top of the water. To do this, you want to heat your water in a pan. While you are waiting for the water to boil, mix a tablespoon of corn starch with half a cup of cold water. Stir until completely dissolved.

Once your water has started to simmer, take off the heat and add the corn startch mixture. Allow to cool and this will be the water you add your acrylic paints to.

WARNINGS!

All the makes included in this book are designed for adults and are not suitable for children under the age of 14.

Keep all ingredients and finished products out of the reach of children.

Some ingredients may irritate; always avoid contact with skin and eyes. If ingredients come into contact with eyes or skin, wash with cold water immediately.

Do not ingest; if accidentally ingested drink water and seek medical advice.

We recommend wearing old clothes or overalls when partaking in creative activities. Cover work surfaces to avoid mess.

TYPES OF PAINT

There are many different marbling techniques and products to try. Here is a quick breakdown of the different types of products you can use:

ACRYLIC PAINTS:

This is probably the most cost effective, easy and least messy of the marbling techniques. The results are permanent and there are so many different colours to choose from.

You can also use primary colours (red, blue and yellow) and mix them together to make even more colours!

To use these, you will want to include Pouring / marbling products.

NAIL POLISH:

Nail polish might be messy and a bit smelly but the results are truly amazing! The drying time is also significantly reduced.

Just be careful, nail polish is really hard to get out and tends to go everywhere.
To remove, simply wipe with some remover and a cloth.

ALCOHOL INKS:

Alcohol Inks work really well and the colours are really vibrant. These can be very messy and stain, so make sure to protect your surfaces and wear gloves.

GENERAL SET UP

WORKSPACE:

You will want to ensure you have plenty of space. We also suggest you use a plastic sheet to protect your workspace and floor. If you are working inside, always make sure you are in a well ventilated room.

PROTECTIVE CLOTHING:

When marbling, small splatters of paint are unavoidable. To avoid ruining your clothing, we suggest you wear an old apron / clothing.

MARBLING TRAY/BOWL:

Your tray all depends on what you are marbling or the paint you are using. If your tray is too big, you will be wasting a lot of ink.
Equally, too small and you won't be able to manoeuvre your items to get good coverage.

CLEAN YOUR BOWL OR TRAY:

Once you have finished marbling, we suggest you rinse your bowl in warm, soapy water straight away. While the paint typically comes off, we suggest you use something that you don't mind getting paint all over.

MAKES
6

30 MINS
TO MAKE

MAKE
WITH KIT
CONTENTS!

MARBLE
STONES

MARBLE STONES

When you find out marbling can be done on almost anything, things get really exciting! For our first make, we are going to marble pebbles. These are perfect for decorations around the home or as small paperweights!

YOU WILL NEED

· Small plate or tray

KIT CONTENTS

· 6x smooth pebbles
· Wooden stirring stick
· 3x acrylic paints

METHOD

1 To begin, make sure you have a clean, tidy space to work in. It is best to have an old cloth ready for any spillages.

2 Next, get all of your equipment ready and close by. As we are only dipping pebbles, you do not need a very wide bowl, as this will only waste the paint.

3 Select your first colour. Now holding your paint pot above your bowl, use your stirrer to gently drop a few drops of paint into the bowl.

4 Repeat the process on the next colour paint, and then again on the last colour.

5 Now, using your stirrer, carefully swirl the paints until you see a marble effect. Be careful not to over stir. This will cause the paint colours to mix, you just want them to gently come together.

6 Carefully drop one of your pebbles into the paint and move the stone to cover all sides. Again, do not roll too much or the paint will mix rather than marble.

7 Leave your pebble to dry before repeating with the underside, alternatively you could leave the underside un-painted.
Repeat with your remaining stones.

MAKES
1

20 MINS
TO MAKE

MARBLE
CANVAS

MARBLE CANVAS

A marble canvas is the perfect, personalised addition to your home decor. What's even better, is that you can hand pick which colours you think will go with its surroundings.

YOU WILL NEED

· Plastic Cup – one for each colour used

KIT CONTENTS

· Acrylic Paint in your choice of colours
· Pouring / marbling medium
· Canvas

1 To begin, make sure you have a clean, tidy space to work in. It is best to have an old cloth ready for any spillages.

2 Next, get all of your equipment ready and close by.

3 Fill one plastic cup with 30ml white paint. Mix with 60ml of Pouring / marbling medium, a splash of water and stir.

4 Now repeat this step, using a plastic cup for each colour you plan to use.

5 We will be starting with white, as this will be the base colour. Take your plastic cup with the white paint and pouring / marbling medium mix and pour onto your canvas.

6 Spread the paint with a wooden stirrer or craft knife. You want to make sure you completely cover the canvas and all 4 sides.

7 Now you want to take the plastic cup with your first colour. Hold it tight in one hand. Use the other hand and select another colour, slowly pour that colour into the other. Then repeat this until all colours are in one cup.

IMPORTANT do not mix the colours. You want them to stay separate.

8 Start to pour the cup with all the colours onto the canvas. We suggest making a figure 'X' shape.

9 Carefully lift the canvas, holding two corners. Start to tilt the canvas left and right, allowing the paint to move across the top. You want to do this until the entire canvas has been covered.

10 Once the canvas is completely covered, put down and leave to dry. It may take a few hours, but the results are definitely worth the wait!

**MAKES
1**

**20 MINS
TO MAKE**

MARBLE
MUGS

MARBLE DIPPED MUGS

This really easy technique is perfect for personalising your mug. By carefully selecting the right colours, you can make a range that sits together and looks incredible!

YOU WILL NEED

- Tray or bowl (big enough to submerse your mug)
- Nail polish remover
- Wooden stirrer
- Cotton pads
- Small craft brush
- Mod Podge

KIT CONTENTS

- White ceramic mugs
- Nail polish in your choice of colours

METHOD

1 To begin, make sure you have a clean, tidy space to work in. It is best to have an old cloth ready for any spillages.

2 Next, get all of your equipment ready and close by.

3 Fill your tray or bowl with warm water. You need enough water to fully submerge your mug.

4 Open your nail polishes and pour into the water. You want enough to cover the top of the bowl or tray.

5 Use your wooden stirrer and swirl the nail polish across the surface of the water.

6 Holding the handle, dip your mug into the nail polish and water. You want to submerge the mug to the level you want the design to reach.

7 Hold the mug in place for 5 seconds. Then, use your stirrer and swirl around your mug, this will pull any lose nail varnish away before you lift your mug.

8 Now, leave your mug on a flat surface to dry.

9 If you're marbling more than 1 mug, you will need to dispose of the current water and start the process again, regardless of whether or not you're changing colour.

10 If you want to make your mug dishwasher safe, wait for it to dry and then add a thin coat of Mod Podge using a small craft brush.

20 MINS TO MAKE

MARBLED
TRINKET DISH

TRINKET DISH

These colourful and vibrant trinket dishes are the perfect addition to your jewellery collection. Colour match to your décor and make them sparkle with a metallic finish.

YOU WILL NEED

- Nail polish remover
- Wooden stirrer, like a Toothpick
- Disposable tray or plastic tub

KIT CONTENTS

- Small white dish
- Nail polish
- Metallic marker
- Optional – Clear spray top coat

METHOD

1 To begin, make sure you have a clean, tidy space to work in. It is best to have an old cloth ready for any spillages.

2 Next, get all of your equipment ready and close by.

3 Fill your tray or bowl with warm water. You need enough water to fully submerge your trinket dish.

4 Open your nail polishes and pour into the water. You want enough to cover the top of the bowl or tray.

5 Use your wooden stirrer and swirl the nail polish across the surface of the water.

6 Holding as little of the dish as possible, dip it into the nail polish and water. You need to make sure the top of the trinket dish is completely submerged.

7 Hold the trinket dish in place for 5 seconds. Then, use your stirrer and swirl around your dish, this will pull any loose nail varnish away before you lift your dish.

8 Now, leave your dish on a flat surface to dry.

9 Once dry, take your metallic marker and draw around the edge of your trinket dish.

10 If you want to add a layer of protection, you can spray your dish with clear top coat.

MAKES 1

20 MINS TO MAKE

MARBLE COASTER

MARBLE COASTER

This really easy make will transform any dinner party. Colour match or mix and match, whatever you decide they will leave your guests asking where you got them from.

YOU WILL NEED

- Tray or plastic tub
- Disposable gloves
- Optional – masking tape

KIT CONTENTS

- Glass coaster
- Alcohol inks in your chosen colours

METHOD

1 To begin, make sure you have a clean, tidy space to work in. It is best to have an old cloth ready for any spillages. The inks can be messy and stain clothes and skin so make sure you protect your worksurface and wear gloves.

2 Next, get all of your equipment ready and close by.

3 Optional – Apply a strip of masking tape to section off an area of the coaster. This will give a clear line and leave a section without ink - it looks great when making a collection of coasters.

4 Carefully pour your first colour onto your coaster. Once done, do the same with the other colours you have, one by one. We suggest you pour these in lines so they don't mix until the next stage.

5 Start to tilt the coaster left and right, allowing the ink to move across the top. You want to do this until the entire coaster has been covered.

6 Once the coaster is completely covered, put on a flat surface and leave to dry.

MAKES
1

25 MINS
TO MAKE

MARBLE
BAUBLE

MARBLE BAUBLE

Create a collection of these simple but striking Christmas decorations that you can keep forever!

YOU WILL NEED

- Foam block or polystyrene
- Wooden skewers
- Disposable tray or protective sheet
- Plastic cups

MATERIALS

- Glass, ceramic or plastic bauble
- Acrylic paint in your choice of colours
- Pouring / marbling medium
- Optional – Clear spray top coat

METHOD

1 To begin, make sure you have a clean, tidy space to work in. It is best to have an old cloth ready for any spillages.

2 Next, get all of your equipment ready and close by.

3 Your first step is to make a drying rack. This will allow the baubles to dry without anything touching. First take your polystyrene block and place on a flat surface. It's a good idea to put this in the place you want to leave it to dry.

4 Now take your wooden skewers and push the first one into the block. Push in as far as it will go, but be careful not to push too hard as you may mark the table underneath. For the next skewer, make sure you leave enough space so two baubles can sit side by side without touching. Once in the right place, push the remaining skewers in place (you should have one for every bauble).

5 Now you want to gently remove the cap on top of the bauble (keep in a safe place). The bauble should now have a hole that will fit on top of the skewer.

6 Now you can start preparing the paint. With your first colour and in an empty cup, mix 30ml of paint with 60ml pouring / marbling medium and a splash of water.

7 Now repeat this step, using a plastic cup for each colour you plan to use.

8 Now you want to take the plastic cup with your first colour. Hold it tight in one hand. Use the other hand and select another colour, slowly pour that colour into the other. Then repeat this until all colours are in one cup. **IMPORTANT**, do not mix the colours. You want them to stay separate.

9 Over a bowl or large plate, hold your bauble in one hand and with the other begin to pour the paint over the top.

10 You will need to rotate the bauble left and right to ensure the paint has the desired coverage.

11 When you are happy, place the bauble on the drying rack.

12 You can repeat this process on as many baubles as you like.

MAKES 2 30 MINS
TO MAKE

MARBLED TEA LIGHT HOLDER

TEALIGHT HOLDER

These coasters are great for adding a finishing touch to your coffee table or bedside, their repetitive nature makes for a relaxing project.

YOU WILL NEED

- Plastic cups
- Spoon or stirrer
- Tray or plastic tub

MATERIALS

- Glass tealight holders
- Acrylic paint in your choice of colours
- Pouring / marbling medium

METHOD

1 To begin, make sure you have a clean, tidy space to work in. It is best to have an old cloth ready for any spillages.

2 Next, get all of your equipment ready and close by.

3 Fill your plastic cup with 30ml of your first colour paint. Mix with 60ml of Pouring / marbling medium, a splash of water and stir well.

4 Now repeat this step, using a plastic cup for each colour you plan to use.

5 When you have all the colours you want to use, pour them one by one into your bowl or tray.

6 Use your spoon or stirrer to combine the colours. Do not mix them together. You want them to stay individual but for the colours to overlay each other.

7 When the paints resemble the marbling you desire, dip your tealight holder into the mixture. Roll them about and use the spoon to get full coverage. Do not over roll as you don't want the colours to mix.

8 When completely covered, remove and leave to dry.

MAKES
1

1HR
TO MAKE

MARBLED CLAY DISH

MARBLED
CLAY DISH

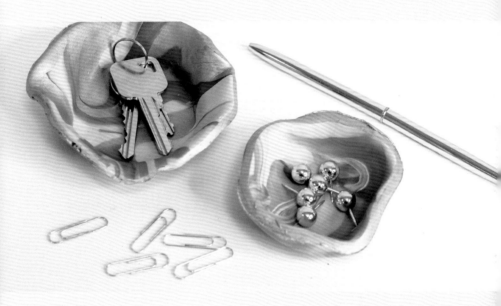

YOU WILL NEED

· Knife
· Rolling pin
· Cookie cutter
  (or something similar)
· Oven safe bowl or
  ramekin

MATERIALS

· Oven-bake clay in
  your chosen colours
· Gold or silver paint
  pen or marker
· Optional – Clear
  spray top coat

METHOD

1 To begin, make sure you have a clean, tidy space to work in. It is best to have an old cloth ready for any spillages.

2 Next, get all of your equipment ready and pre-heat the oven as per the instructions on your clay pack.

3 Cut a chunk of clay for each colour you have chosen – pick the ratio depending on what colour you want more or less of.

4 Each chunk of coloured clay needs to be rolled into 12cm rods. Roll it between your palms to soften the clay, until a rod forms.

5 Twist all of the different coloured rods together and roll into a 25cm rod, using the same method as step 4.

6 Fold the rod in half and then twist together again.

7 Repeat rolling, folding, and twisting 2-3 more times

8 Squash the twisted clay rod into a ball - what you see on the surface of the ball will be your pattern.

9 Using a rolling pin, roll out the clay ball until it's 3mm thick and in a rough circle shape.

10 Cut out circles using a cookie cutter or cut out around a can or other round template (one circle = one dish so make as many as you'd like!)

11 Place the circle evenly into a bowl or ramekin that is a little smaller than the circle. It should sag a little in the centre and result in a dish shape.

12 Once the oven has reached the required temperature, put the clay dish on a tray and bake as per the instructions for the clay you have bought.

13 Remove the bowl from the oven and allow to cool. To remove, turn the bowl upside down and tap lightly until the clay dish falls out of the ramekin.

14 Once completely cool, use a paint marker or small paint brush to colour the rim of the dish, then set aside to dry.

15 If you desire a glossy finish, seal the dish with clear glossy spray paint following the instructions on the can.

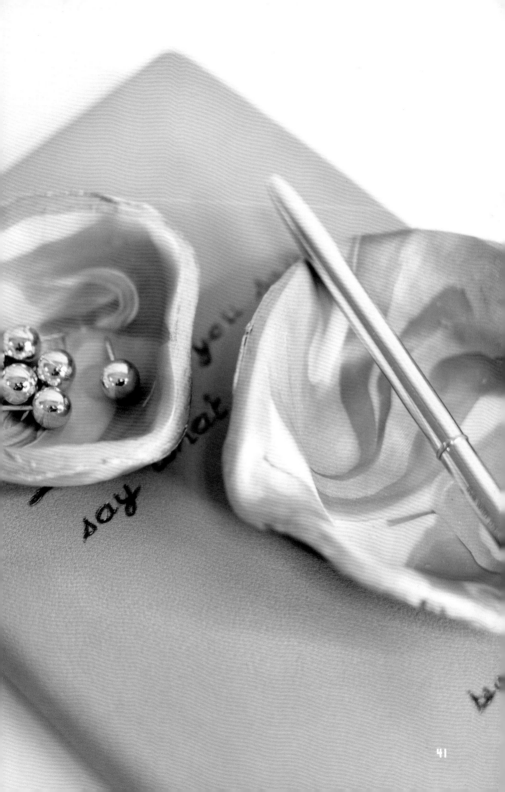

**MAKES
1**

**30 MINS
TO MAKE**

MARBLE
PLANT POT

MARBLE PLANTER

These marble plant pots give your plants a whole new meaning. By adding a splash of colour, you can transform a fireplace, window ledge or any part of your home!

YOU WILL NEED

- Wooden stirrer
- Plastic cups
- Disposable container or plastic tub

MATERIALS

- 2-3 x acrylic paint colours
- White acrylic paint of your choice
- Terracotta pots
- Optional – Clear spray top coat

METHOD

1 To begin, make sure you have a clean, tidy space to work in. It is best to have an old cloth ready for any spillages.

2 Next, get all of your equipment ready and close by. The bowl you use will depend on the size of plant pot you are colouring. Remember it needs to be big enough to dip the plant pot into the paint.

3 Select your white paint. Now holding your paint pot above your bowl, use your stirrer to gently drop some paint into the bowl. The amount you need will depend on how big your plant pot is. You may need to estimate and add more if you need it later.

4 Repeat the process on the next colour paint, and then again on the remaining colours.

5 Now, using your stirrer, carefully swirl the paints until you see a marble effect. Be careful not to over stir. This will cause the paint colours to mix. Remember you just want them to gently come together.

6 Carefully dip your plant pot into the paint and roll slowly to cover all sides. Again, do not roll too much or the paint will mix rather than marble. If you have a big plant pot, you may need to use a spoon to pour some of the marbled paint on top.

7 Once your plant pot is covered to your desired amount, place in a safe spot to dry.

**MAKES
1**

**15 MINS
TO MAKE**

MARBLE
PAPER

46

MARBLE PAPER

Marble paper is great for scrapbooking, picture frames or just for fun. You can pick your own unique colour combinations and create as many sheets as you like. No matter what colours you pick, each one will be different to the last and you will end up with a selection of one of a kind designs.

YOU WILL NEED

- Tray or plastic container
- Wooden stirrer
- Kitchen paper or paper towels

MATERIALS

- Alcohol inks in your choice of colours
- Watercolour paper

1 To begin, make sure you have a clean, tidy space to work in. It is best to have an old cloth ready for any spillages.

2 Fill your plastic tub with approx. 1 inch of water.

3 Start to add your alcohol inks to the water, one drop of colour at a time.

4 Try dropping the inks inside the previous colour and around the edge to vary your pattern – you can experiment on this step!

5 You can also try stirring the water with a wooden stirrer to further mix the colours.

6 Once you're happy with the design you have, carefully place your sheet of paper on top of the water so that it has full contact with the water and there are no air bubbles.

7 After the paper has absorbed the ink, carefully lift the paper from the water surface and leave on some paper towels or kitchen paper to dry.

8 You can continue to use the same water and add more alcohol inks to create your next sheet.

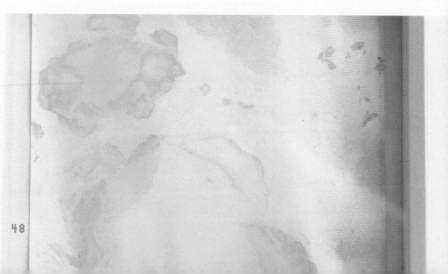